Autonomy and Altruism

Lauren Smith

Presentation by *BookLeaf Publishing*

Web: www.bookleafpub.com

E-mail: info@bookleafpub.com

ISBN: 9789363316706

First edition 2024

I dedicate this book to anyone who has ever suffered with mental illness. Our brains can be torturous creatures, of this I know. I never thought I would break through, but I have, and I lovingly wish the same for you.

ACKNOWLEDGEMENT

I want to acknowledge and genuinely thank deeply those of my support system who motivated me through this process. Thank you for teaching me how to share my words and be proud of my journey. You know who you are!

When I First Met Joy

This is sitting in the discomfort
Not building a home for it to grow over like
wildflowers, no,
It's more like inviting it to sit down together for
tea.
It's knowing that I am it, and it is me.
It isn't wrong to feel, but it's asking me to see
I was not meant to drown in fear.
Sometimes it can feel like a long time, one year
But it's only barely a fraction of the years I've
lived here
Came back to ground, buried my hands in the
wet soil and begged for mercy that tasted like
bliss
The spirits told me it would hurt more than I
could envision before the sun would finally greet
me
I remind them no amount of pain would make
me want it any less
And that the shadows cuffed to my wrists
prepared me for the transition
Like when I felt the first shadow of despair lift
from my eyes
Given the clearest of skies to see from
We could see for miles and miles

But it was only a glimpse
As everything else is,
A property of change
But we would meet again

Path of Forgiveness

Opens entrances to doorways I didn't know
existed
Lets windows fly open that were,
for all I knew,
sealed shut with no way of opening
Forgiving means seeing the heart within
someone else past their mistakes that hurt you
Witnessing the child within them who hurts the
same way that I do
Cries the same tears that I let loose
Forgiving opens a portal to mirroring each other
past the circumstances that bind you
Releases you out of the pain that blinds you
Because I do,
I want what's best for you
It isn't me and I'm living with it
moving with it
breathing with it
You forgiving yourself means more to me than
holding onto my pain or justifications
Although it did hurt to be hurt by you -
I release it in the spirit of moving forward
Closing the chapter
Just don't write me off as heartless before you
understand

the truth behind the decision to let us go
I want to let the windows bring sunshine into my
soul like I've never known before
I want the sunshine for you, too

Jimmy Really Does Eat Wednesdays

Dancing in the middle of a 7-Eleven downtown
Eating pizza on the curb at 2 AM
You didn't even want it,
You just didn't want our time to end
Neither did I
Hugging me after we sang emo karaoke
Everyone cheered and your hand on my low
back
Both made my heart race
Making fun of you for drinking Malibu and
Coke
Listening to music in your car until 5 AM
I had so many songs to show you
Fast forward one week
Gasping at the full moon while we sat on a
cooler together on a boat tour
Eating tamales with green sauce
Then getting peed on by bats
There is nothing else I would have rather been
doing
No better way to see this city
And get to know your heart
Something in you welcomed something in me
home

I bring color to your eyes
And you bring music to my ears

I Vowed Not To Give Up On Myself

When my inner child starts the rage within my heart
Ignites the fire
I let it burn
I let her feel it
Screaming to be let out of this body through words
in a voice even I have never heard
I hold her in times of perceived loneliness
Feeling like she just doesn't have this life thing figured out
Was it ever meant to be figured out anyway?
Mostly, she doesn't think so
How subjective
So badly wanting to grow out of this numbness
Make sense of this overwhelm
Feel held by the magic hands of the Universe
To know what I want and why
To know,
Something doesn't need to be wrong all the time
There's beauty in the unknown
There's strength in picking up our own pieces to rebuild ourselves wiser
We're all perfect as we are

We have come so far
We can do this

Self Love in the Branches

When I turn to ash
And get planted as a forest tree
I will still hope you're rooted next to me
In the ambers
Spring time and in winter
The five o'clock ticket gets you sunset ready
Will you ever be ready?
A tiny strong human overlooking a mountain
peak
So much smaller than we think
Our feelings will run like ink,
If we would just let them
Getting to know ourselves under the vast starry
sky
Close our eyes and soak into the minerals
The rocks at your feet
Stepping into it
Show up as you are
There's no more turning away
Be a part of your own life
Because you are here to stay
Write how you feel and whisper it to the wind
Tell the world of your hurt and it will throw
paths for healing directly at you
Ask the universe for what you want

It only wants to provide for you
It is all temporary
So make yourself known
And be your kind of kindness
Play in the wind
Sing and dance
Laugh at the jokes your friends tell about you to
others
Let the love in
Until it consumes you
Then start spitting it back out
As if it was always yours
It is, always yours
I am, always yours

Limitless Color

The smooth rock gliding over
my winter brushed fingers
sent me back to a time
when searching the grounds for the smoothest
collection of rocks
to marry with my acrylics
Was in the top favorites of a way to spend my
days
Such a simple time
Before due dates
Before heartbreaks
Before I knew what presence was and yet, I was
just it
Effortless, knowing nothing less
than getting lost with brushes
Rinsed into a rainbow in my mason jar
Before thoughts of the future filled my mind
And worries of who I was haunted me
It was just painting rocks simply
Making them whatever I wanted: clouds or turtle
shells and the familiar smells of acrylic paint fill
the spaces in between
when I thought I got too old for it all
Trying to grow down now -
Slow down now,

back to small space and,
brush strokes and,
simpler times
When looking back wasn't filled with questions
and looking forward,
It just wasn't necessary yet

Chains of the Season

The tree leaves fade from bright green to soft
amber
as the fall days approach winter
The sun still rises
making its way slowly out of the fog and gray
clouds that fill the morning air
As i sip warm coffee that keeps my own
cloudiness at bay,
for the time being
The four walls that hold me while I sleep are
waking up and breathing now
They gently nudge me to
Do the same,
wake up and find the air outside.
I pull out my old, often untouched, bicycle
Sweep off the cobwebs that had been collecting
and making my stationary tool a temporary
home
I leave home,
not the first time,
not the last.
Once the tires hit the pavement, I leave the night
in the past
The necessity to pedal forward,
or we fall down

Such is life isn't it?
Can I ride my bike and think of you at the same
time?
I keep my face toward the sun and capture the
way the trees change in shape and color
as my body and bicycle pass by them
Life has changed in shape and color-
since learning how to ride this thing,
yet the skill is never forgotten.
Funny how some things just stick with us
Forgetting myself, I keep riding
I pass a tree blasting the scent of lemons
I stop to pick
only a few
And I make love
and sweet lemonade

A Sunset and A Promise

She has grown before her own eyes like the
wildflowers growing on the edges of the streets
Tall and moving with the wind
The light of the sun beams through her fingertips
as they move in the breeze
She knows this air that keeps her alive has her
back through all eternities
And her eyes have seen pain, but the trees hear
her cries and bring a soft comfort of rain
The wind says "this will be okay."
The soil promises her bones that peace is here
The future is clear
And the angels had been telling her she was a
poet for a while now
Its peaking it's way through her curious rib cage
made of coconut milk and lavender
She sees that art was a missing link
A practice of expression with no wrong answers
She once believed all of her answers were wrong
But that's because she didn't see the promise
between the roots of the trees Intertwining
underneath her bare feet
Always traveling with her and always of support
She may have bought the first few lies
When her brain told her she was bad

But the sunlight now welcomes her to walk the
world hand-in-hand
The truth has taken stand
With the trees that sway side-by-side
A family of land
And she is the baby

It All Comes Together

They said wait
For the moment when all the pain starts to make
sense
When the movie of your world starts to roll the
credits and reveal how much work you put into
fighting through and finding healing
To finding this moment,
this feeling.
It's juices marinate my bones
Instead of push it all away, invite it in
and it dances with you.
Let the pen be a reminder
You made it every day to be here now.
You can't run from the fountain of youth and be
drinking at the same time
Why run at all anymore?
At some point,
running was all we knew,
but when we stopped running -
This was when roots grew.
They wrapped around my ankles and took hold
Not letting go until until I promised to slow
down,
open my hazy eyes,

And see the beauty of the day I was waking up
numb to
The truth is,
my heart doesn't feel empty anymore
Or I, incomplete
I knew the valleys in my beating chest could
never be filled with the breath of another.
Or the kind words of a mother,
they would mean nothing until I dug deep
enough to reach the wounds of rotting
foundation
And reconstruct the base from which I was built
upon
Replace the sharp corners with softer edges,
and my tears may fall the same way,
But now they glisten in the sunlight
Instead of drown me.
I'm glad to be loved
I realized that I always was, I just couldn't feel it
until I cracked my heart open
Until I reincarnated as a tear drop on my
mother's cheek
I don't yearn for you to weep for me
And it wasn't until I realized that I was so afraid
of letting go
That it was why I never held on in the first place

The Matter Would Not Be Smooth

Whatever we could do
The matter would not be smooth
All she had to do was breathe
Let the music come to her
She did not have to cry, beg, hide
Fit into someone else's expectations
But there's differences now
It is not the same
No need for shame
In accepting the truth
You accept all of you, too
You see what's held you back in life
Is depending on how others perceive you
How they hurt you or they love you
To such extremes it brought you out of yourself
Fear became regular
But this was years ago
The present is a healed mirror
Miracle
of the way you wanted to deeply leave life years
ago
And now you have nothing but joy in your heart
for being in this lifetime
at this time

right here right now
That contrast is significant
But it is not all,
You drive faster than anyone I know
You howl at the moon
You remember how your heart used to hurt
So you can spend your life feeling less of that
and more love
More more more more more more more more
love
Handcuffs taken off
You broke the cycle of leaving yourself behind
You care how you feel
The state of the world
You care how it feels
The ways you were caught up in your heart
The ways you would tire at your own growth
Clocked your 40 credits
By twenty seven
You grew your self understanding to be safe in
who you are
And it has been years since you realized no one
can tell you that your feelings are wrong
They are YOUR FEELINGS
It's been years

Pendulum

I swing back and forth
Above the sky that's heard all of my stories
Under the water who has listened to my cries
I write this in joy
For the understanding of what is
but the patience in knowing,
I don't know anything
I think of families
Come and gone
Core memories
Intertwined through the vines and whispers of
the trees who stand near me
Life has been a wild ride
I will still sleep outside
I don't always know what life is asking of me
But I have promised I will stay to listen
The universe created me knowing I might be it's
most fragile child
And this wildly capable heart has endured
wildfires
but sleeps to the sound of rain now,
I still wipe the nightmares off my eyelids
But I will stay to listen
I heard somewhere once:
it would be safe to start looking back eventually

your memories would unfold for you like the
petals bloom
asking for your attention now
landing right on your shoulder while you're
praying to the sun
As if to say, "you're ready now,"
but also, "can you take us with you?"
One by one, and never on your own accord

Nana

If I stare too long into the distance,
my eyes dip back into your house on Bonham
Your velvet chair sat caddy corner to the
window
And my spot was always on your lap or your
armrest
Crossword puzzles
Pumba always wanted to play,
your giant poodle
chasing me around the house
Laughter filling my belly
As he tried to nip at my ankles with his teeth
Reba McIntire and corn dogs with mustard
bring me right back to being a kid with you
Riding in the front seat of your white Buick
Century
Maroon interior
On Saturdays we went to garage sales
That we had found the night before in the
newspaper
You called it junking
It was our quality time
Finding old treasures together
Coming home for a nap in your silk sheets
I can still smell the Noxema in your bathroom

You stayed vibrant and silly as hell until the end,
Nana
Your mind loosened up, but your spirit never did

Soulmate, 20 years later

I'm 47 and you're 52
I wake up every morning to a kiss on the
shoulder
I put my face in your armpit to get a big sniff
We've never left our bed without a kiss and I
love you
Just as drunk in love as when we were sang
karaoke
We were calling ourselves old then but we feel
younger now
And we don't even know how, but we're even
happier than when we thought we couldn't get
any happier
Our kids are teenagers,
but the days we held them for the first time
never slips our mind.
They love to sing,
seeing as they got your instrumental genes,
but they paint with me.
We give them opportunities we didn't have at
their age
and it makes everything worth it to watch them
be happy and kind and pay it forward
You're still forward
With me when we get any chance to be alone

You touch me like it's the first time and still say
my skin is the softest thing you've ever put your
fingers on
After all this time, I still believe you
They told us the magic would fade
But I have loved you just as hard everyday
It doesn't fade

See Yourself

These words
Strong like artifacts when I have my own back
Do I dare admit the way the tension releases?
When I bring word to paper and tempt attempt to
re-read it
I pressed rewind
Just long enough to forget that it's mine
So I can love it to the same degree
That I would love it if it was someone else's
I ask the moon for the reasons that it must work
like this
She says,
"Just. Keep. Writing.
It helps the sky breathe,
when you stop clenching your own lungs
and release those fists that hold your voice
hostage."
Within a moment I suddenly recall it all
The big charade life is made of
I weep out
Seep out the effects of taking it all so seriously
Until my wells run dry
I have no more need to cry
I'm reminded of my wholeness again
I surrender the heavy baggage and the stories-

the illusions,
For much too long I allowed the lies to live on
me rent free
Never questioning the pain that was not mine to
carry
So I rejoice
In the moment of remembrance of who I was
meant to be
Bliss ever so free
Creative, loving being
And I hug myself for enduring the forgetting so
long this time
And a few more tears are shed
We have ridden this wave long enough to know
that the tide of self doubt will inevitably flow
this way again
But never in the same form
Peace will find its way ashore
More familiar than the time before

Nassau

I arrived at Viking beach
Across crystal clear blue waves
palm trees that said hello to me
Setting my stuff down on a hostel bed
the world was spinning through my stomach
Reminded me that I asked for this
Completely incomplete in an unfamiliar country
so that I could practice finding my home within
The irony
I could stay locked up inside my room
or I could take these open eyes and see what this
world is about
when I take the focus off of me
Reality-
When the woman who checked me in told me,
she was tired of the heat and wanted cold a cold
place to stay
I remembered the way I shivered at home
And realized we get so accustomed to the things
we have
So we yearn for the things we don't.

A Decade Down

10 years of friendship
We came together in the name of loafers and
arch supports
Tiny teenage bodies, big hearts, and a sea of
shoes
We clocked our two hours a day
After school
We traded as many stories as we could about
what our lives were like
We didn't know a mutual sole-
There was something unique about that
We bonded over simultaneous heartbreaks
and the struggles of dreaming up a world so big
While tied up in a tiny town that didn't smile
very often
We almost got a two-bed two-bath two-story
apartment for six hundred and fifty dollars
but I just couldn't sign myself to stay where I
had always been
I needed to go
You helped me pack my car of all I owned
Took the 10 hour drive with me to the far edge
of the same state
We hit the road with the 806 in our rearview
At least for a little while,

At least for me
and we cried when we said goodbye
It was different than any heartbreak,
More like a dull ache
That didn't fade with time
That was the price to pay for a sole sister
Fast forward eight years and we have done just
about everything together
Growing in our own beautiful ways,
but still sharing every win and every heartbreak
We built homes in a new city several years ago
Our front doors were 5 feet away from each
other, I cherished it.
I will never forget the ways your silly heart
helped my sad heart get better and better
and better
Or the stupid shit we did
Like getting a U-Haul stuck in a ditch
Learning to find our voices
The laughs and the tears
They will always be everything
My pocket of sunshine

Use Your Hands

I think it's about finding our inner child
and walking with them again
Because it's safe here for both of you now
We heal hand in hand because we did not want
to be in pain
Kept choosing love
It's okay that you hit your head sometimes along
the way -
you only meant to make your way
to wherever felt like you were meant to be
Hard to make a plan when you're merely trying
to find your socks and shoes
But it's not the way it is anymore -
You write the plot.
You create your story.
The things that used to work for the life you
were living
no longer serve you now
The pain of the past gives you courage to keep
building a life
with safety and love in it
Get out of your head
Get it on canvas. Put it in clay.
Pour it on keys and strings
Keep choosing life.
It will keep choosing you

Life Bearers

I live through a time where body autonomy is
ripped form the hands of women-
The very hands that create life
are given no choice in the matter
No voice
No decision
Told to figure it out
and make better decisions
I hold the hands and hearts of every women in
this grief
of our rights as they get pulled out from under
our feet
If I could wipe every tear and hold every cheek
What an indescribable step taken backwards but,
You are supported
There are resources
You are not alone
Please know this

I Will Note

It took a while to write because the words were
not easy to find
They were not speakable
And I could not read them back without
squinting
Squirming
And that's the thing I love most about writing
It's permanent
But destroyable if you own it
So know that what I write is truth
Absolute truth for me ~
From the only eyes that I see out of
Know that there is a happy ending
But also no ending at all
As there's no such thing as forever
But there is such thing of permanence
If you're holding this book, it means these words
are permanently out of my
body and mind
Forever in my heart
Temporarily in your hands
May your feelings be safe
Intertwined with the pages
It is my hope that these words seal your heart
back up from brokenness

So that all you feel is eternal love

Internal love